The Lion

Had No

Stripes

Fasa
Eghujovbo

Achievers Publishing Inc
Calgary Alberta

THE BEE THAT HAD NO STRIPES

Copyright © 2015 By Fasa Eghujovbo

ISBN: 978-0-9918829-8-4

Published in Canada, by
Achievers Publishing Inc

Canadian Cataloguing in Publication (CIP)
A Record of this Publication is available from the Library and Archives Canada (LAC).

For further information or permission, address:
Achievers Consult & Publishing Inc
Calgary, Canada
E-mail: info@achieverspublishinghouse.com
www.achieverspublishing.com

Printed in Canada for Achievers Consult & Publishing Inc

Dedication

THIS BOOK IS DEDICATED TO
EVERY PERSON WHO EVER FELT
DIFFERENT

Acknowledgement

There is no other person that deserves more praise about this than my Father in heaven. You were the one that always stood by me and never let me fall. You gave me this idea and made my dream a reality. I just want to thank You for giving me this opportunity.

Secondly, I want to thank my mom and dad, Victor Eghujovbo and Queen Eghujovbo, and my kid sister Efe Eghujovbo. They pushed me to finish this book even though sometimes it was hard. I really want to thank you guys. But mostly, I want to thank my mom. She helped me and guided me through this whole experience and I just want to thank her for that. She encouraged me when I needed it the most. I love you dearly with all my heart.

Finally, I want to thank my mother and father in the Lord, Pastor Sunny Adeniyi and Deaconess Fola Adeniyi of Winners Chapel International Calgary. You are truly special to me. I want to thank you for your support and encouragement you gave me to start this book and finally publish it. Thank you for your prayers and support.

I deeply acknowledge my publisher: Achievers Publishing Inc and my editor: Ruth Yesmaniski for editing the manuscript. Thank you for your assistance.

This book would not have been possible without these wonderful people God put in my life. I am just so grateful for all of you and the wonders and blessings you have given me. May God continue to strengthen you and keep you through the times you need Him most, in Jesus name. Thank you and God bless.

Introduction

Bumblebees - the life and soul of our environment. They collect the pollen to produce honey for us humans. Although, we've never seemed to wrap our heads around the fact that something else goes on inside the bumblebee world, they are things that are quite similar to things that happen in the human world. Different things though, too. Things that we just can't explain. Take you and me for example, there must have been a time in your life when someone has made fun of you for the way you looked. I know I have experienced it before. Now, imagine that same thing happening not with humans but with bumblebees. Now do you believe me? It does sound a little crazy but something like this has happened to a bumblebee before. I've heard about her story a couple of times.

The story of that bumblebee has helped me personally to love myself for who I am and to cherish my uniqueness. I'm sure that if you're having this problem of low self esteem, this story will definitely cheer you up. This bumblebee's name was Leila.

Leila was the, prettiest, smartest, most perfect bumblebee that you could ever meet. She loved her looks. She definitely had the best fur in all of the bumblebee clan. She was, unfortunately, very proud and never cared about what anyone said to her about it. In her school, Leila was super popular. Every bug in the school wanted to be just like her, in every way possible. You see, Leila didn't just associate with anyone, for her to even look at you, you had to be at the top of the hierarchy. But Leila did occasionally talk to the "unpopulars." However, that was only when she was doing her charity work. Leila's version of charity work was when she encouraged other bugs to change their looks so they could look more like her. She knew it was wrong but she wanted to be a role model to other bugs. There were some bugs that didn't like her too. It's not that they didn't like her looks, it was that they didn't like her attitude. Leila could be a pretty rude bug.

Everyday, Leila would take the bus to school. But before the bus came, she would spend time complimenting herself in the mirror. She would say, "Leila, you're beautiful, popular, and smart. Who doesn't like you?" Leila was a very confident bug. She always knew that she was better than everyone else and she never forgot to show it.

The bus finally arrived and Leila headed off. Leila was so popular that she had a special seat in the bus just for her. It was in the front of the bus. It had a perfect leather finish and the wind blew directly through her fur from the window. She always sat at that very spot and no one could take it from her.

Once Leila finally got to school, she met up with her friends at the front of the school.

"Hey girl! You look perfect as always," Leila's friend Samantha said as Leila approached her. Samantha, one of Leila's best friends, was the organized one of the group. She always handled everything that had to do with Leila and her friends making appearances at places to where she and her friends sat at lunch. Samantha sometimes did get a little jealous of Leila but she would never show it.

"I know. I used a special honey perfume today. It's super expensive and no bug has it yet. What do you guys think?" Leila was the type of bug that fished for compliments. She wanted bugs to compliment her. It made her feel superior.

"You look and smell so sweet. That perfume is golden," said Rebecca, another friend of Leila's. Rebecca was the perky one of the group. She was crazy, literally. She was also never afraid to try new things. But even with her crazy attitude, Rebecca was the sweetest out of all of them.

After talking for a while, the girls finally entered the school. As they flew down the hall, bugs were awestruck in their presence. Every bug in Southern Bug School wanted to be just like them. Bugs copied their style and trends. If you didn't wear what Leila wore, you were an outcast.

As Leila and her friends flew down the hall, different bugs approached them. One bug flew straight up to Leila and said, "Hi Leila! I took your advice and got my fur cut like you wanted me to."

"That's great Hazel. Now you can look more like me," Leila giggled and her friends laughed with her. Hazel didn't seem impressed.

"Oh um, right. I guess I'll see you guys around then." Hazel flew away.

Leila and her friends got to their lockers. All of their lockers were located side by side. They were also the biggest and the best lockers in the school. That was what they had requested from the principal of the school. And of course, they had to listen to her. Leila had power. Leila could get someone expelled with a whip of her stinger. That's why nobody messed with her. It was because of her father, who designed the school. If his princess didn't get what she wanted, there would be issues with some teachers' pay raises.

"You were totally doing Hazel a favour back there Leila," Rebecca blurted out.

"Ya I know. She just didn't seem as excited as we were about it."

"Whatever. She's an "unpopular". It doesn't matter," Samantha added.

The first bell rang and Leila and her friends had to get to class. They all started flying to class when another bug came flying towards them.

"Hey Leila, Samantha, Rebecca. You guys are still coming to my party right?" Dmitri was the school jock. He was the most athletic, most popular, most handsome guy in the school. He also threw the best parties every year to celebrate his birthday.

"Ya definitely. We'll be there," Samantha made a note on her phone for the party.

"You still want us to sing right?" Leila asked.

"Yes that would be perfect. Thanks Leila." Dmitri flew away.

"He totally likes me!" Leila shrieked. They all laughed and flew to their class.

The day finally ended and Leila headed home. Apart from Leila's success in school, Leila also had favour with her parents at home. Leila was the "All-star" bug. Her parents loved her for her excellent marks, excellent attitude and excellent heart. Well, that's how they thought she acted.

Once Leila got home, her parents welcomed her with open arms.

"How was your day honey?" Asked her dad. Leila's father was a home designer. He designed different nests and gardens that bugs lived in and he was extremely good at his job. That's why their nest was so big and beautiful.

"It was really good actually. I got an A plus on my Science test."

"That's great Leila!" Her dad said.

"I hear someone got an A plus on a test. Pick anything you want for dinner," Leila's mother exclaimed. Leila's mom was a professional chef. She cooked for lots of bugs for parties and get-togethers. Leila's lunch was always the best at school because of her mother's excellent cooking skills.

"Surprise me," Leila answered. She flew upstairs to her room to freshen up before she ate dinner that night. As she changed, she heard loud music coming from outside. She looked out the window to see her sister drive up to the nest and fly into the house. Leila's older sister was someone Leila looked up to. Leila's sister was flawless, literally. She was a cheerleader in her school and everyone adored her. Everything she said and did always made sense. She was awesome.

"Leila, dinner is ready," her mother hollered from downstairs.

"Coming mom!" Leila finished changing and headed downstairs.

Everyone sat down at the table and had an awesome time. They all talked and laughed and shared stories about their days and how they had gone.

"So I did Hazel a huge favor and she didn't even thank me," Leila acknowledged as she finished her dessert.

"Well, what did you do for her?" Her mother asked.

"I told her to get a haircut so she can look better."

"Leila, that's kinda rude don't you think?" Leila's sister, Hannah, claimed.
"No its not. I was doing her a favor!" Leila shot back.

"You were telling her to change the way she looks. That's not right," Hannah answered.

Leila was infuriated with her family. She couldn't believe that they didn't support her on her journey to help the bugs that seriously needed help. "Well, I think

I'm done my food. I'm going to my room."
Leila got up from the chair she was sitting
on and flew upstairs to her room not
looking back for one second.

It was finally time for Leila to get to
bed. She didn't think her day could have
gotten any better. As she flew into her
room, she caught a glimpse of a shooting
star in the distance. She hurriedly flew to
her window and sat on the ledge. "I wish,"
Leila thought for a while, "I wish nobody
could be like me. Ya, they can look like me
and talk like me, but they can't be me. I wish
I can become so unique that bugs will copy
my style without me even telling them to."
Leila was very confident about her wish.
She just knew it was going to come true
even if she didn't really believe in shooting
stars. She then went to take a quick shower
and headed to her bed. Leila loved her life
but she just wanted it to be a little bit
better. But the best part was the freedom

that she had to do whatever she wanted to do.

The next morning, Leila woke up late. She flew out of bed. She needed to get ready fast or she would be late for school. She hurried to the bathroom to take a shower. Leila knew she could not be late for school so she had to go as quickly as possible.

"Leila! Leila come downstairs you're going to be late!" shouted Hannah from down the stairs.

"I'm coming! Just tell the bus driver that I'm going to be a little late," replied Leila.

As Leila was getting ready for school, she noticed that she felt a little different than she did the previous day. She didn't notice it as much but something inside of her felt out of place. But that didn't stop

Leila from getting down the stairs still looking and smelling like perfection. She grabbed her bag and flew as fast as she could down the stairs not bothering to look in the mirror before she left.

"So, what's for lunch?" Leila asked her mother as she was getting breakfast ready.

"Well, I have put together a very special lunch today to reward your A plus in school," Her mother said, facing the stove. When her mother turned around, her eyes widened. Her mother's face turned from cheerfulness to confusion as she looked at her daughter from head to toe. She dropped the honey on the floor.

"Mom? What?" Leila had a very astonished look on her face, she didn't know what happened to her mom or why she was looking at her like that.

Her mother stared at Leila with her jaw dropped to the floor. "What......?" her mother's voice was shaky. She just stood there, frozen, and stared.

Leila was amazed. She had never seen her mother act like this before. Her mind immediately thought of her wish last night and how she had a weird feeling earlier in her room. She didn't know how to react.

Hannah then flew through the door. She stopped and looked at Leila. She didn't know what to say. "Okay. What is going on? Is this some kind of joke Leila?"

Leila frowned. *Do they think her appearance was a joke?* she thought. She didn't know what was so wrong.

"Leila, what did you do?" Her mother finally said.

"You tell me, cause I don't know," Leila asked.

"Your black stripes are gone!" Hannah yelled.

Leila gasped. Her stripes were gone? She rushed to the bathroom to check the mirror. Her family was right. All of Leila's stripes had disappeared.

The bus honked. Leila was already late for school. She didn't want to go in the first place. If bugs saw her looking like this, they would freak out.

"Um, Leila, you have to get to the bus. You're going to be late," Hannah said as she approached Leila in the bathroom.

Leila didn't know what to do. She wanted to cry but her body wasn't letting her She wanted to scream but she couldn't find the breathe to. She just stood there in silence. Jaw opened wide, not saying a word.

Leila had to make a decision. She finally said, "I'm not going to school. I just want to stay home to figure this out.

"Absolutely not," her mother barged in. "You are going to school even if you don't have any stripes."

Leila disagreed with her mother. She couldn't go out looking like this. She had a reputation that she needed to keep. But her mother didn't care. She dragged her out of the bathroom and out the door. Leila was shaking. *My life is ruined,* she thought. With no stripes, she would be an outcast. No one would want to copy her style now.

As her mother pulled her out of the bathroom and out the door, all that was going through Leila's mind was negativity. *What will other bugs think? Will I still be popular? What will my friends think?*

Leila got to the bus. She took a deep breath and flew unto the bus. The chatter on the bus ceased instantly. Bugs were staring at her and it made Leila very uncomfortable. Even the bus driver was staring.

Leila stood for a while then flew to the back of the bus. She shrunk into the back seat and tried to look as invisible as possible. A bug flew up and sat right at Leila's signature seat at the front of the bus. Leila felt horrible. The bus began with a jolt and the kids headed off to school.

The bus was quieter than it usually was in the mornings. Bugs would take quick glances at her, then turn away when Leila looked at them. Some bugs didn't even care if Leila saw them look at her, they just stared. Leila felt like an outsider. A prisoner in her own world. As other bugs entered the bus, nobody bothered to sit next to her on the bus.

Lots of bugs were whispering things like, "What happened to her?" or, "Is that really Leila?" Leila was heartbroken. The bus finally came to a stop and they were as late as ever. Leila flew off the bus quickly to see if her friends were waiting for her at the front of the school. Nobody was there. Now Leila was worried. If her friends weren't at the front of the school, that meant everyone was already inside. Everyone would see her. She knew what everyone would think and say.

Leila flew into school slowly and silently. The noise in the school promptly stopped. Every bug of different shape and size stared at her. She tried not to make eye contact with anyone. She spotted her friends. Their jaws dropped. Rebecca whispered, "Leila?"

Leila felt terrible. She wanted to go home. She knew it was a bad idea to come to school today. Some bugs were even laughing at her and mocking her. Leila couldn't handle it. She was humiliated. She flew straight to the bathroom, closed the stall door, and cried.

The first bell rang and Leila needed to get to class, but she was too depressed to even go. She flew out of the bathroom stall and started flying to class.

As Leila got to the door, bugs started to stare at her. She ignored them and sat at the back of the classroom. Rebecca came to sit beside her. "What happened to you?" Rebecca asked.

"I don't know. I just woke up like this," Leila answered. She was glad that someone wanted to talk to her even if she looked different.

"You should have stayed home. I mean, don't you notice everyone staring at you?" Of course Leila noticed. She hated it.

"Ya, but what can I do? I would stare at myself if I could." Leila felt good that her friend wanted to talk to her. No one had talked to her all day.

"Right. Well I need to get back to my seat. Class is about to start," Rebecca started to fly off.

"Wait there's a seat right here if you want," Leila pointed to the seat beside her.

"No thanks. I like to sit at the front of the classroom." She flew away.

Leila knew that Rebecca didn't come to talk to her out of kindness. She knew that Samantha put her up to this just to see what was wrong with Leila. That's the kind of bug Samantha was. She always sent other bugs to do her dirty work.

The whole day for Leila was a disaster. Nobody sat with her at lunch, nobody wanted to be her partner for projects and nobody talked to her. The only thing bugs actually did was stare at her.

The day was finally over and Leila didn't feel any better than she did in the morning. She felt worse. The bus ride home wasn't a bed of roses either. Still as quiet as the morning bus ride. Most bugs didn't pay her very much attention now. They didn't see her as a threat any longer. Leila hated that.

Leila got into the door of her nest and slammed it shut. Her father and mother both jumped at the sound. Leila threw her bag on the table and her books on the counter. She really didn't want to deal with her parents and their drama today, after all she had gone through at school.

"How was your day honey?" Her father asked.

"How was my day? Well I don't know Dad. Why don't you ask everyone in school who laughed at me and stared at me, ask them, not me because I really don't want to talk right now," Leila wanted to cry again.

"Oh, Leila. Its okay," her mother flew over to her and gave her a hug.

Leila brushed her off and flew upstairs to her room. Even though she didn't want to admit it, she did really need a hug from her mother right now.

Leila needed to do something about her complexion. She couldn't experience what she experienced today again. She sat on her bed and thought, *how can I change my appearance so I can look like I looked before?* She thought, and thought, and thought until it hit her. She can just paint on her stripes. A smile spread across her face. She grabbed her paint trays and filled them with black paint. She then grabbed large paint brushes and got to work.

Leila stayed in her room painting for a long time. Nobody downstairs bothered about Leila and what she was doing. They all left her to do what she wanted to do. But her mother was getting worried. After a long time her mother finally said, "Leila, you've been in there for a long time now. May I ask what you're doing in there?"

"Nothing you would be interested in," Leila yelled back. She had a rush of adrenaline inside of her. She was so ready to strut her stuff in school on Monday so everyone could see her new and improved stripes.

"Leila, you have to come downstairs now. You've been in there for too long," said her father.

Leila was ready to show her family her stripes. She spent a long time in her room for a good cause and now she was ready to show them what she was doing. She flew downstairs. When her family turned to look at her, they were in shock.

"Your stripes came back?" Hannah said with amazement in her eyes.

"Um, not exactly. You see, I was in my room for all this time painting my fur so it would look like I still have my black stripes when really I don't. Smart, right?" Leila waited for their response. Hannah just shook her head and went back to eating her food again. Her parents didn't look very impressed either. They all went back to eating their food not paying Leila any attention.

"Hello, my stripes are back!" Leila was so angry with her family. She couldn't believe that none of them were paying any attention to her. One minute they were pleased and the next, they don't even notice her.

Everyone was silent until Hannah said, "Leila, that's cheating. You can't just paint on your stripes and expect everything to be happy go lucky again. All you're doing is making yourself look like someone that you are not. It's not cool. Take my advice and cherish your uniqueness."

Leila was speechless. Her sister knew the torture that Leila had gone through that day. She knew that even her friends turned against her. Leila frowned. She thought none of her family members were being considerate. "I can't believe none of you care about my feelings. None of you care about what I went through today. It's not fair!" Leila was furious. She hated how her family looked at her and she hated how they acted.

"Leila, of course we care. But instead of trying to change it, learn to accept it. It isn't that bad you know," Leila's father said.

"Whatever!" Leila flew upstairs to her room.

The next day was a Saturday. Leila was feeling very tired and she didn't want to get up. She finally got out of bed and went to the bathroom. She had the craziest dream that night. Her dream was very repetitive. Bugs were laughing and making fun of her even though she was extremely popular. In the dream, Leila didn't have any stripes. She hated that dream and she never wanted to have it again.

As Leila looked in the mirror and saw her reflection, she realized that this was no dream. It was reality. Leila frowned. What she hoped was only a dream was turning into her own nightmare. She just couldn't bear it any longer.

Leila had to do something about this, apart from painting on her stripes, she had to figure out why she, out of all the bumblebees, had to loose her stripes.

"Mom," Leila began, "Can we go to see a doctor today?"

"And why on earth do you want to see a doctor?" Leila's mom asked.

"I want to figure out why I lost my stripes," Leila quickly answered.

"Well, I don't know. I guess we can." Leila's mom didn't seem very excited about it but she pulled through and agreed to let Leila go to the doctor.

"I'll be outside," Leila said as she flew out the door.

As soon as they got to the office, bugs started to stare. Some of the stares were of fright, or horror. Some were even of shock. Leila shrank into the corner of her mother trying to stay out of sight as best as she could. They both sat down in the waiting room and waited for the doctor to approach them.

A tiny little bee stared at Leila with big rounded eyes. "Mommy, why does that bee look weird?" The bee asked in confusion.

Leila shot the bee a mean death stare and the bee tensed up like a stone.

"I am so sorry. Little bees and their big mouths," the mother chuckled. Leila didn't seem to find that very funny but Leila's mother smiled and went back to reading her magazine.

After a long wait for the doctor, he finally arrived. He escorted Leila and her mother to a room filled with all kinds of scary and colorful experiments. Leila was instructed to sit on the chair and wait for the doctor to return. Even though Leila didn't want to, she did it just for the sake of getting closer to finding the cause of her loss of stripes.

"So, Leila. What seems to be the problem?" The doctor asked innocently.

Leila wanted to laugh. "Seriously?" She asked. She didn't think doctors could be so stupid.

Leila's mother gave her a cold stare.

She shivered. "Um, I lost my stripes."

"I see," the doctor began to think. "Miss, was there anyone in your family before that also lost their stripes?" Asked the doctor.

"Not that I remember," Her mother answered. She thought for a while. "Oh wait! My uncle, Paul. He lost his stripes from getting attacked by a human, I think," Her mother said.

Leila was confused. Was her loss of stripes related to the loss of her mother's uncle's stripes? She was never attacked by a human before. She had never even left the clan before.

"Bingo," the doctor smiled. "The reason that you, Leila, lost your stripes was because of your uncle that lost his stripes in the past. It's like a genetic thing. If someone in your family has already lost their stripes, someone in the family is guaranteed to lose their stripes in the future. Unfortunately, you were the one to lose them."

Leila felt terrible. The person that had to lose their stripes in the family had to be her. She was devastated. "So, is there any way I can get my stripes back?" Leila asked.

"Well, not really. Since it's a genetic cause, there is no real medication that can give you your stripes back. But, if you wait a while, they might just come back again."

Leila was speechless. The doctor was telling her to accept the fact that she had no stripes and move on. She couldn't do that. She needed her stripes back now.

Her mother thanked the doctor, left the building and headed home. Once they got home, Leila immediately rushed to her room. She looked in the mirror and frowned. *I can't wait until I'm back to normal again,* she thought. She thought of all the bugs that laughed at her and called her weird. All the bugs who she called friends, just like that, thought she was an outcast. It hurt Leila a lot. She just couldn't bear it any longer.

Throughout the rest of the weekend, Leila thought about her condition. She thought about her life before she lost her stripes and how it was perfect. She had the best grades, and now she barely made it to school. She had the best friends, but they stopped talking to her. And she had the best looks, but now she was a nobody. But what could she do? It wasn't her fault that her stripes went away. It was her mom's uncle's fault. She hated that bug for doing this to her. She hated everyone for making her feel this way. She just wanted to get away. Leave everything. Then the words her sister said to her at the kitchen table came flooding into her mind again. "Cherish your uniqueness." She never really knew what those words meant. They were just words to her. She knew that she had to accept the fact that she might not have anymore stripes but she just couldn't do it. She wanted to be back to normal and fast.

The weekend was finally over and school started again. Leila really didn't want to go to school that day. She knew that everyone was going to laugh at her again. As her mother flew up the stairs to ask Leila if she was ready to go to school, Leila let out a loud cough.

"Leila, are you okay?" Her mother asked with lots of pity in her voice.

"I think I'm sick mom. I don't think I can go to school today," Leila lied. She coughed again to add emphasis.

"Oh dear. Well you can't go to school when you're sick. Stay home. I'll call the school to tell them you're not feeling too well," her mother added.

Leila felt a jolt of victory flood through her veins. She succeeded in not going to school. "Thanks mom," Leila moaned. When her mother left, Leila was happy. At least she had another day to think about everything before she had to face the world again.

For the whole day, Leila felt guilty. She wondered about all the things she was missing that day. Then she remembered all the bugs that stared and laughed at her. She could never seem to get their voices out of her head. *Leila? What happened to your stripes? Why do you look so weird? I thought she was popular. Is that the same Leila from a day before?* She wondered what was going through Samantha and Rebecca's minds when they saw her. *Is she okay? We can't talk to her when she looks like this. What is wrong with her?* What about Dmitri? *What happened to her? Should I still let her come to my party?* She suddenly remember something. The party. She promised Dmitri that she and the girls would sing on that day. But how was she suppose to sing in front of the whole school when everyone thought she looked weird? She had to call the girls, even if they weren't on very good terms at the moment.

First she called Rebecca, but she didn't pick up her phone. Then she called Samantha.

"Hello?" Samantha paused for a while. "Leila?" Samantha was extremely surprised to be hearing from Leila after all this time.

"Hey Samantha! What's up?" Leila asked with a shakiness in her voice.

"Um, nothing really. Are you okay, you sound afraid," Samantha said.

"I'm fine. I was just sick today. By the way, did I miss anything important in school today?"

"No. We didn't learn anything new," Samantha sounded very confused. "Hey I was meaning to ask you, what happened to your stripes?"

"Um, well, since my uncle lost his stripes in the past, someone in the family had to lose their stripes eventually in the future. Unfortunately, that bug was me," Leila answered. She didn't really want to talk about that at the moment.

"Oh, really? Because I heard that it was a punishment from God or something because he was trying to teach you to be nicer to everyone," Samantha laughed.

Leila was offended. Bugs were already starting to make up rumors about how she lost her stripes. She knew that that was not okay. "Well, that's not true."

"Okay then. Well I have to go right now," Samantha really didn't want to talk to

Leila at the moment. She didn't want others to see that she talked to her.

"Wait! I called you for a reason," Leila cried.

"Okay. What is it?"

"I wanted to ask you if we were still singing for Dmitri's party?"

Samantha was quiet for a while then said, "Well, since you weren't here at school today, me and Rebecca asked Hazel to fill in for you so we could practice and stuff. Surprisingly, she is really good. So since you don't look like yourself and I don't think you're even going to go to the party anymore, we just asked Hazel to sing instead of you. No hard feelings though. I mean, it's not like you're not a good singer. It's just Hazel is available."

Leila didn't know what to say. She was replaced by an "unpopular". She was furious. "Oh. You could have just called me Sam, just to ask if I'm still going to sing with you guys."

"I know. We just didn't think you would pick up. But I mean, we're sort of doing you a favor. Now you don't need to bother going to the party or showing your face. Now bugs won't laugh at you."

Leila tried to hold in her anger. She knew that if she did start yelling at Samantha, the whole school would know about it.

"It's a win -win for everyone Leila. You look different from everyone else and nobody likes you right now. If you don't want to make a bigger fool of yourself, don't go to the party." Samantha blurted out.

Leila couldn't contain herself anymore. Samantha had gone too far. "What do you mean 'if I don't want to make a bigger fool of myself?' I am not a fool! Nobody can call me that, not even you! And I'm going to that party whether you like it or not! I am not going to sit here and let you or anyone for that matter push me around like I'm some sort of toy! I'm sick of it!!" Leila was furious. She wished Samantha was in front of her right now so she could yell at her face.

"You know Leila, you really haven't changed. I thought maybe losing your stripes would give you a little sympathy. It obviously didn't. You're worse than you were before. And do you know what I have to say: you're ugly now, inside and out. With you losing your stripes, all it has done is made me more popular, and that's what I wanted all along. So thanks for making my dream come true." She paused, "I hope you never get your stripes back." Samantha hung up the phone.

Leila was very angry at Samantha. She knew that Samantha was going to tell the whole school that she yelled at her. But she didn't care. She was going to that party even with no stripes. She had to prove to Samantha and the rest of the school that she was strong. She could take their criticism.

Leila looked in the mirror again. She remembered what she told herself each morning before she went to school. *Leila you're beautiful, popular and smart. Who doesn't like you?* None of the words she said before she believed now. Before, she was beautiful, popular and smart. Before, no one hated her. But now, she was different.

Leila went to sit on her bed. She was in a very depressed mood and she really needed someone to talk to. She flew over to

Hannah's room. She heard Hannah talking on the phone to one of her friends so she couldn't talk to her. Her parents had just left the house too and they weren't coming back for a while. Leila went back to her room and sat down. She needed to talk to someone about everything that had happened.

Leila felt a sudden urge in her spirit to do something that she hadn't done for a very long time. She needed courage to talk to this person; she was afraid that he wouldn't listen. She knelt down beside her bed, closed her eyes and bowed her head. She started to pray. "Well, I don't know how you're suppose to start these things," she began. "I mean, I haven't done this for such a long time but I guess I'll give it a try again.

"There has been a major problem in my life for some weeks now. I've been really confused on what to do about it. I'm guessing You already know what I'm talking about. I've lost my stripes. Since my stripes have disappeared, it's been nothing but the worst for me. Bugs have been really mean and cruel to me. When it first happened, I got into school that morning and everyone stared at me and laughed at me. Even my friends turned against me just because I was different. And what really sucks is that I'm feeling worse and worse every day about it. And I know I can waste all my time and my money just trying to look like myself again, but something in me is always stopping me. Something in my spirit is helping me go through all of this. I don't know what it is, but I'm pretty sure it's you. I just want everything to go back to the way it was before, when everyone liked me and respected me. I don't know if you could do that, but God, you're my only hope. I don't think I can take another day of the stares. I've become so depressed and alone. I just need someone to talk to me again.

"There's a party on Saturday that I want to go to. I just don't know if I should. It's not for my own fun, but to prove to everyone that I can handle everything they say to me. I can be strong. I'm really having mixed feelings if it's a good or bad idea though. What should I do? Should I go to the party, or should I stay home?" Leila paused and waited for an answer. She heard nothing. She thought maybe she said something wrong.

"Um, I sort of need an answer, God," Leila reminded. She still heard nothing. She felt that God didn't hear her. Maybe He didn't want to tell her to go or not. She opened her eyes.

"Leila it's time for dinner," hollered Leila's mom from downstairs.

"I'm coming mom." Leila uttered a silent "amen" then headed downstairs.

"What were you saying in your room upstairs Leila? Have you lost so many friends that you've gone to the point of talking to yourself?" asked Hannah with a rude tone in her voice.

"I was not talking to myself. What's wrong with you today," Leila replied with the same tone in voice.

"So what were you doing in your room Leila?" Her father said to break the ice between his daughters.

"Oh, I was praying," Leila answered.

Hannah dropped her fork. "Praying?"

"Yes. Is that a crime in this house?" Her family's faces had the look of astonishment. The last time her family prayed was ages ago. They didn't even go to church.

"Well, no its just, we haven't prayed in so long and I didn't think you would be the one to bring it back," her father added.

"Well I needed God to help me with a situation so I prayed. No big deal." She wondered why her family was so surprised that she prayed.

"Well, that's wonderful then!" Her mother said with excitement. "You know, Leila is setting a very good example for this family to follow. We should start to pray more often. In fact, let's pray right now!"

The whole family held hands together except Hannah. Mother shot her a look and she quickly held hands with Leila and Dad.

"Hannah, why don't you pray for us," Mom asked.

"Um, dear God," Hannah began, "Thank you for this food that you gave to us and thank you for what you've done for us. Thank you for my parents and my sister, and thank you for our amazing house that we live in. Amen."

Everyone said "amen" all at once and began to eat their food. Mother was smiling and that made everyone else smile too.

After dinner, Leila flew upstairs to her room. As she was going to her room she paused when she got to Hannah's room. She stopped and entered her room.

"Hey Hannah, can I talk to you for a second?" Leila asked.

"If it's about what I said at the table, I'm sorry. I was just in a bad mood," Hannah answered.

"No it's not because of that, but thank you. It's actually about everything that has been happening to me lately. You have a minute?"

"Ya, what's up?" Hannah was all ears for what Leila had to say. She felt as if she needed to tell Leila something that would help her at that party.

"Well you know all these things that have been happening to me, you're right. I don't have any more friends. They replaced me with an "unpopular". I feel like no one understands me anymore. I wish everything just went back to the way it was before. My life was better then than it is now. And now, there's Dmitri's party that I don't want to go to but I'm afraid bugs will think I can't take their criticism and hatred and they'll only laugh at me more. I really don't know what to do. I need some help."

Hannah was silent for a moment then finally said, "Leila, maybe losing your stripes wasn't a bad thing. I mean, since you've lost your stripes, ya, bugs have been bullying you, but you're learning to accept yourself for who you are in more ways than one. You really have grown as a bug and as an individual. The bugs that were your friends don't know what they're throwing away. They are getting rid of a superstar. You're a superstar Leila. Don't you mind what anyone says about you. You're way too good for them. You're the most popular girl in school and everyone knows that. Always remember that. You are awesome just the way you are. So go to that party. Show them who's boss. Cherish your uniqueness!"

Leila smiled. Every word that Hannah said made Leila feel so much better than she did before. "Your right. I need to grow a stinger and go to that party. I don't need to care about what bugs think of me. Thanks Hannah. That helped a lot."

"Ya, no problem. Goodnight Leila."

"Goodnight Hannah." Leila went to her room, closed the door, and went straight to bed.

The dreaded day finally arrived. It was a Saturday and Dmitri's party was that night. Leila was more ready than ever to go and show all those bugs what she was made of. She got dressed and was ready to leave when she caught a glimpse of herself in the mirror. She stared at that image staring back at her for a long time. She finally said, "Leila, you're beautiful, popular and smart. Who doesn't like you?" She felt as if she could take on the world that night. She was confident and prepared for whatever would come her way. She took in a deep breath and flew downstairs and out the door.

When Leila arrived ,just the outside of the nest looked amazing. Dmitri had really outdone himself this time. Inside, it was even better. The lights, the music, everything was perfect.

As Leila flew inside, bugs started to stare. Leila didn't even mind it, she was used to all the stares already. She just flew right past them, with shoulders held up high, and continued on her way. She was looking for Samantha and Rebecca. Her "ex" friends. She was ready to confront them about the issue at hand and show them who was the boss around here.

They were by the stage with Hazel, getting ready to perform. When they saw Leila, their faces filled with surprise and shock.

"Oh, Leila. I didn't think you were going to show up. After the argument," Samantha scowled.

"Well I did. And now I need to tell you guys something that I didn't have time to say on the phone," Leila waited for them to respond but no one said anything. All they did was cross their arms and look at her.

Leila began to speak. "Ever since I came to this school, I've been popular. We've been popular. There was nothing that tore us apart. We ruled the school because of our popularity and we had the best of everything. Now, looking back at my life before, I realized that it wasn't the life I was supposed to be living. I was a fraud, and a fake. Through this whole experience of me losing my stripes, I've never missed my life before. In fact, I think the life I'm living now is a whole lot better than the life I was living before. And the first day I lost my stripes, I didn't realize it. I let everyone bully me, I let you guys insult me and make fun of me. But no more. I'm a new bug, and a new individual. And I'm not going to let anything you or anyone else says bring me down anymore."

Leila's friends were shocked. They had never heard Leila speak like this before. But Leila's friends were not only shocked, they were amazed. No one had ever had that much courage to talk to the popular girls like that, but Leila did.

They were silent for a while until a bug came up to them and asked them if they were ready to go up on the stage and sing.

Leila looked at the bug then looked at her friends. Hazel smiled and handed Leila the microphone. "You deserve to go up there, not me. Break a leg," Hazel hugged Leila and flew away.

Leila and her friends flew up onto the stage. The crowd went silent. Bugs were whispering and laughing and no one seemed to pay them any attention. Leila's confidence was draining. She didn't know what to say or what to do. She felt alone again. She felt like everyone turned against her. Then the words that encouraged her to come to the party started flushing into her head. *You are a superstar. Show them who's boss. Your beautiful, popular and smart. Who doesn't like you? Cherish your uniqueness Leila, you can do it.* Leila was feeling empowered, alive, confident. It was like happiness was flowing through her veins and ready to gush out of her at any moment.

Everyone stared at her, waiting for Leila to say a word. After a long time of waiting and staring, Leila finally said, "It took a lot of guts and courage for me to come to this party today." Everyone was still silent. A bug in the crowd yawned. Leila frowned. That didn't stop her though. "Who here has ever been made fun of for the way you looked or acted?" No one answered. The crowd was still and silent. Then suddenly, Rebecca raised up her hand. Everyone's attention was directed on her. Then Samantha raised up her hand. Bugs stared at them. Leila smiled. Then Hazel raised up her hand, then Dmitri, and just like that, every bug in the room raised up their little hands and encouraged Leila to keep on talking.

"Who here has been told you're not good enough?" Everyone's hands were still raised up high. Leila was filled with joy. Maybe bugs did care about her, even without her stripes.

Leila directed the crowd to put their hands down then continued to speak. "For the past weeks, I have been trying to deal with losing my stripes. At first it was a shock to me. I couldn't bear the fact that I might not be popular again. I was bullied, humiliated, and laughed at. Even my friends ditched me because they found a better option that came along. I thought my life was over. I thought I would never be happy again. But, I am standing here today to tell everyone that that isn't the case. Since I've lost my stripes, I've become stronger as an individual. I can now fly out in public even without stripes.

"As my stripes were disappearing, I was thinking that the bug I was inside was disappearing as well. But, I'm still me. Just a better, nicer version. The bug I was before can never compare to who I am now.

"This whole experience has really taught me a lesson. It taught me to cherish my uniqueness. I know I'm not super popular or perfect any longer. But being a bug that doesn't care what others think is much better than popularity and perfection.

"And after all this, I guess what I'm trying to say is that we are all different. And it's ok. Everyone who raised their hands today should be proud. You showed yourself that you don't care about what others think of you. We should be proud of our flaws not try to change them."

The room was silent. Then a small applause started to erupt. After a while, every bug in the room was cheering and screaming and clapping for Leila. Leila smiled. She knew in her heart that all of this wouldn't have been done if it wasn't for God. Maybe He did answer her prayer.

Then the music began to play for Leila and her friends to sing their song. Leila began to sing first, "Sing to the world tonight, show them what's beautiful. I don't care what they think, no I'm not listening, cause I know I'm beautiful."

As Leila sang the words to that song, she felt amazing. She had never felt the feeling of real joy before, until tonight. Everything was perfect. The song, the party. And every bug that ever stared or laughed at her, instead praised her. Even though she was not super popular anymore, she still had friends that loved and cared for her. And that's all that mattered.

Leila learned a very valuable lesson that night. Even with her haters, she still stood strong. She learned to cherish her uniqueness and love the body God gave to her, even if to others it wasn't all that great.

When Leila got home that day, she felt so much better than when she left the nest.

"How was the party Leila?" Her mother asked when Leila flew through the door.

"It was perfect mom. Just like everything about me. Perfect." Leila had a huge smile on her face. "And mom, I'm sorry for the way I've been acting lately. It hasn't been right and I'm sorry. Will you forgive me?"

Leila's mother laughed. "Of course Leila. I'm just glad that you're back to the daughter that I know and love."

Leila hugged her then flew upstairs to her room. She sat by the window. Again, she saw a shooting star. She closed her eyes and wished upon it. "I wish that nothing would change. Everything is perfect." The star drifted away and Leila crawled into her bed. She fell asleep peacefully and quietly.

On Monday, Leila felt refreshed and renewed. She was ready to take on the world. It was the first school day for a new bug. The new Leila. Leila got ready for the day and before she exited her room, she looked in the mirror. Instead of saying her usual phrase each morning, she said, "I am perfect just the way I am. I don't need bugs' opinions to be happy. I'm my own bug. And I'm proud of who I am."

When Leila got to school, bugs welcomed her with open arms. They were cheering and smiling at Leila. She met up with her friends at their lockers and they greeted her.

"Hey Leila! How was your weekend?" Samantha asked.

"It was actually very peaceful. Thank you for asking. How was yours?"

Rebecca was the one to talk this time. "It was great!" She said. "You know everything you said that day at the party meant a lot. I mean, we all go through our lives judging others when we don't take the time to judge ourselves. You changed a lot of our lives that night."

Leila felt warm inside. She didn't know that she changed lives that night. She smiled and they went on their way to class.

Throughout the day, Leila helped bugs around the school find their inner beauty. She talked with them and helped them. Leila felt excited to tell her parents all that had changed about her that day. As soon as she got home, she told her parents all about the changed Leila.

"Well, maybe losing your stripes was a blessing in disguise," Her mother said.

"I definitely agree," added Hannah.

That night, before Leila went to bed, she knelt down beside her bed and closed her eyes. "Dear Jesus," She began. "I just want to say thank you. Thank you for showing me that's its okay for me to be different. Thank you for giving me the confidence to go to that party. Thank you for changing me. I couldn't be more grateful for what you have done for me. I've become the bug that you want me to be. And I couldn't ask for anything more. Thank you God for answering my prayer. Amen."

From that day forward, Leila became very well known in her school and around the hive for the kindness that she showed to all bugs. Everyone loved her even without all of her stripes. Any time any bug needed help solving any issue, Leila was the one to call. Leila became more popular than anyone that had ever been in her school, even more popular than her sister. But Leila didn't use her popularity for evil, but for good. And she had losing her stripes to thank. I mean, if she hadn't lost hers stripes she would be the same bug she was before.

Leila's life has completely changed over the past few months. She has realized that all her life, she hadn't appreciated what she had until it was gone. She never realized that she had to care about what was on the inside rather than on the outside. But what really mattered was her heart and what she thought about herself.

And that's Leila the bumblebee's story. I told you it would make you feel better. Since then, Leila has never forgotten the encouraging words that she heard all around her: "cherish your uniqueness." Maybe you're a different skin color than those around you. Maybe you're super smart and others think of you as a nerd.

Maybe you have a mental illness and people make fun of you. Growing up is about discovering your unique gift and not following the crowd. Most times, we are afraid of getting teased and laughed at. We all want to be liked, be accepted, be loved. But does that mean following the rest? It doesn't matter if you're big or small, or short or tall. You matter. It doesn't matter what others say about you. You're perfect. It's okay to be different and it's okay to be something new. You're beautiful just the way you are. So the next time you feel like you don't matter or you're not unique, think of Leila the bumblebee and how she learned to love herself for just the way she was.